Museums for 'The People'?

Institute of Ideas
Conversations in Print

Museums for 'The People'?

By Josie Appleton

With Robert Anderson, David Barrie, Maurice Davies, Richard Fortey,
David Lowenthal, Timothy Mason, François Matarasso, Sue Millar,
Charles Saumarez Smith, Ian Walker

This edition first published 2001 by Academy of Ideas Ltd.
Signet House
49-51 Farringdon Road
London EC1M 3JP

ISBN 1 904025 01 3

British Library Cataloguing in Publication Data
A catalogue record for this book is available from
the British Library

Designed by Joe Ewart for Society
Back cover photograph by Niall Sweeney for Pony
Printed by Futura Printing Ltd.

T

Institute of Ideas
Expanding the Boundaries of Public Debate

Conversations in Print

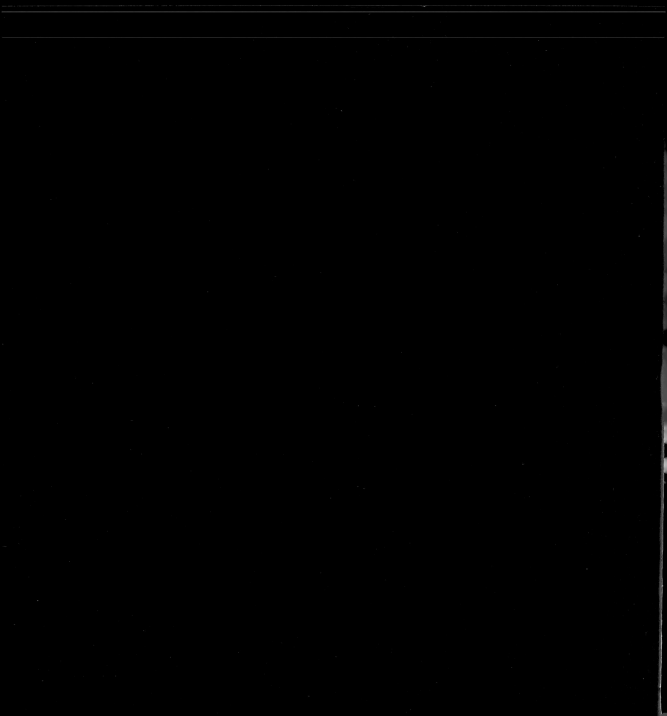

Contents

Introduction

The origins of this **Conversation in Print** go back to the Culture Wars conference held in London in March 1999. The conference was organised by what was then LM magazine to discuss dumbing down in the arts, education and the media, and particularly the way in which the charge of elitism was being used to silence criticism of highly controversial policies. At the conference, we organised a number of sessions on museums. To our surprise, the subject aroused some of the strongest passions, among both curators and museum-goers. In the months that followed, many of the debates and discussions we held, often on quite unrelated topics, had the uncanny habit of coming back to this subject. So many of the problems which arose in other areas of culture seemed to find a particularly strong and concentrated expression in the world of museums. Among museum professionals, the inner sense of confidence in the direction and purpose of their work was shot to pieces.

To shake certainties and challenge the orthodox view is of course a vital part of any culture. The history of learning consists of just such radical challenges to the received wisdom, each new generation putting its elders to the test and in turn having its own orthodoxies defied. The manner in which the old orthodoxy is challenged however reveals so much both about the honesty and vitality of the culture as a whole. Open debate, in which the truth of rival claims can be tested and assessed, is a sign of a healthy cultural life. But no such debate has taken place in the museums' world. Instead, the vacuous slogans of relevance, accessibility and inclusiveness went up like a monotonous whine, drowning out dissent. Officials would give speeches, all cut and pasted from each other. Professionals would stand up in meetings and mouth the new litany of phrases.

This was the new orthodoxy, and anybody who didn't wholeheartedly embrace it was an elitist, a snob, or even a racist.

This was a culture of conformity, unhealthy and oppressive. People would express in private their concern at the dumbing down of museums and then either say nothing in public or worse, repeat the dreary dogma they had just castigated in private. Then there is the furtive squeeze of the arm after a meeting, and someone whispering in your ear: 'I'm so glad someone said that', as much as to say, 'I've always thought that myself, but I daren't say it'. Sometimes the interlocutor will vanish as if he fears being seized by men in leather coats.

Was this oppressive conformity coming from the government? Certainly the Department for Culture Media and Sport did not improve matters with its bureaucratic support for the new orthodoxy. Nor can the increasing financial dependency of the arts on the state be healthy. But New Labour is not the Inquisition. Quite the opposite in fact: criticism can often lead to promotion. It was a convenient fiction to blame the government. All the problems within could be displaced onto an identifiable external target. It was comforting to believe that if only the government would drop all its bureaucratic quota-filling and target-setting and give museums the money they needed, everything would be fine.

There is little that's new in any of the Blair government's policies or proposals for museums. New Labour did not invent the idea of museums becoming campaign centres for cultural diversity, social inclusion and self-esteem. Nor did the government invent the idea that since all collections are ideological, why not abandon the pretence of objectivity, and turn museums into instruments of 'good' multicultural ideology.

Museums all over the country were doing that well before May 1997, and the so-called 'New Museologists' were advocating such things since at least the mid-80s. Many in the museums' world might recoil from some of the consequences of recent years, but there has been little criticism of the underlying orthodoxy.

Josie Appleton's essay is a daring critique of the new established order in museums. No doubt she will win both friends and enemies. For the Institute of Ideas, the most important thing is to have the debate, open and uninhibited. Many people, of varying shades of opinion, have already contributed both their ideas and their support for our work. Thanks to all of the contributors to this book, for engaging in the discussion and responding to Appleton's essay.

I would particularly like to mention the British Museum and its Director, Robert Anderson. In July 2000, Dr Anderson very kindly hosted the 'The Social Responsibility of Museums' conference, organised by Josie Appleton, on behalf of the IoI. He has always been most generous in his thoughts and his criticisms. I would also like to thank Maurice Davies of the Museums Association. As you will see from his response, Maurice has little sympathy with the views either of Josie Appleton or of the IoI. Yet he has been most gracious in helping to raise the debate. To Marc Pachter, Director of the National Portrait Gallery at the Smithsonian Institution, our thanks for his unstinting support over the years. Many a time we have benefitted from his fine historical sense and the broadness of his vision. I would like to extend a special thanks to Michael Daley, Director of ArtWatch UK. In his disinterested love of art, he is a fine example of what it is to be a custodian of culture, while his incisive thoughts have always brought clarity and good sense to our discussions.

Finally, thanks to Joe Ewart for the design of our Conversations in Print, and his indefatigable support of our work, and to Dolan Cummings for his editorial assistance.

Mark Ryan
Institute of Ideas
October 2001

9

Biographies

Josie Appleton is a writer for the online current affairs magazine spiked (www.spiked-online.com). She has written articles on museums for the *Spectator*, *BBC History Magazine*, *Museums Journal* and the *Independent*, and has spoken about the new consensus in museum policy at a number of conferences. In July 2000 Appleton coorganised a conference on 'The Social Responsibility of Museums' at the British Museum, part of the month-long Institute of Ideas series of events. Appleton holds an MA in Latin American politics and has a special interest in ethnic movements.

Dr Robert GW Anderson has been Director of the British Museum since 1992. He was educated at Oxford, completing doctoral research on inelastic neutron scattering in 1970. From Oxford he went to Edinburgh where he was a curator at the Royal Scottish Museum moving to the Science Museum in 1975 where he became Keeper of Chemistry. He returned to Edinburgh as Director of the National Museums of Scotland, developing the concept of the Museum of Scotland and selecting the architects. This opened in 1998. At the British Museum, the Great Court, designed by Norman Foster and completed in 2000, has been the main focus of his work.

Anderson's research and publication, which he has struggled to maintain, is concerned with Enlightenment science on the one hand and the history of museums on the other. Currently he is editing the correspondence of the chemist and industrial consultant Joseph Black (1728-99). He has been President of the British Society for the History of Science and of the International Scientific Instrument Society. Honorary doctorates are held from Edinburgh and Durham. He is a Fellow of the Royal Society of Edinburgh and an Honorary Fellow of his old college, St John's.

David Barrie was born in 1953 and studied Experimental Psychology and Philosophy at the University of Oxford before entering the Diplomatic Service in 1975. He served in various posts in the Foreign and Commonwealth Office and Cabinet Office, at the British Embassy in Dublin, and was seconded in 1989 to become Executive Director of The Japan Festival 1991, a major celebration of Japanese culture that took place throughout the UK. In 1992 he was appointed as Director of the National Art Collections Fund, a charity that helps museums acquire works of art and acts as an advocate of museums and their visitors. An expert on Ruskin, his publications include an abridged edition of John Ruskin's magnum opus *Modern Painters* (revised edition, 2000). He is a Director of The Guild of St George (a charity founded by Ruskin which is responsible for the Ruskin Gallery collection in Sheffield); a Trustee of the Ruskin Foundation (which is responsible for the Ruskin Library collection at the University of Lancaster); and was Chairman of Ruskin To-Day (the co-ordinating committee for the Ruskin Centenary in 2000). He is a board member of Re:source: the Council for Museums, Archives and Libraries, and a member of Re:source's Acceptance-in-Lieu Panel.

Maurice Davies is deputy director of the Museums Association, an independent, non-governmental membership organisation that supports and represents museums and people who work in them. He has worked as an art curator at

Manchester City Art Galleries and Tate and was editor of *Museums Journal* for six years. He has lectured at many universities including Cambridge University, Imperial College, universities of East Anglia and Leicester. He is involved in many museum-sector initiatives and is a member of the Ministerial Advisory Panel on Illicit Trade and the DCMS Human Remains Working Group. He has a degree in pure maths from the University of Warwick and a doctorate in art history from the Courtauld Institute. He is a very inactive member of the Labour Party. He strives not to work full time and his main out-of-work activity is caring for and entertaining two young children.

Richard Fortey is a senior research palaeontologist at the Natural History Museum, London, and a writer on evolution and geology. For many years he was responsible for the care and curation of trilobite fossils in the national collections. He has published more than 150 scientific papers on matters scholarly and geological. He was the recipient of the Frink Medal of the Zoological Society of London in June this year in recognition of his research and writing. *Life: An Unauthorised Biography* was shortlisted for the Rhone Poulenc Prize in 1998, and his latest book *Trilobite! Eyewitness to evolution* was shortlisted for the Samuel Johnson Prize for Non-Fiction. He has served as a judge for the Rhone Poulenc Prize, and on the Committee for the Public Understanding of Science (COPUS).

David Lowenthal is Emeritus Professor of Geography at University College London. A graduate of Harvard (1943),

Berkeley (1950), and the University of Wisconsin (1953), he taught history and geography at Vassar College, was a Fulbright Fellow at the University of the West Indies, and was Research Associate, then Secretary of the American Geographical Society in New York. He has been a Guggenheim and a Leverhulme Fellow, is a medallist of the Royal Geographical and the American Geographical societies, and a Fellow of the British Academy. His books include *West Indian Societies* (1972), *The Past is a Foreign Country* (1985), *The Heritage Crusade and the Spoils of History* (1996), and *George Perkins Marsh: Prophet of Conservation* (2000). He has been a consultant to the Science Museum, the Victoria and Albert Museum and the British Museum, and in 1999 gave that museum's third annual AW Franks Lecture, 'White Elephants and Ivory Towers: Embattled Museums?'

Timothy Mason is a cultural consultant with substantial experience of the arts and heritage, both in the UK and abroad. He is experienced in managing major cultural organisations, well known as a writer and lecturer, is a frequent broadcaster and has served on several national, Commonwealth and other international committees. As a consultant his clients have included Kent County Council, the Department for Culture, Media and Sport, the Heritage Lottery Fund, the Fundación Antorchas (Argentina), QUEST, the Arts Council of England, ICOM UK and the Georgian Group.

Between 1995 and 2000 Mason was Director of the Museums and Galleries Commission and prior to that was Chief Executive of the London Arts Board. He has been the Director of the Scottish Arts Council and of the Western

Australian Arts Council. He has had extensive professional engagements abroad including in western and eastern Europe, Canada, the United States, New Zealand, Australia, Hong Kong, Barbados, Singapore and Argentina.

Earlier in his career Mason worked in the performing arts, including the Royal Exchange, Manchester, Ballet Rambert, the Actor's Company, the World Theatre Season and the Oxford Playhouse.

François Matarasso is a writer and researcher whose work on cultural policy embraces the arts, libraries, museums and heritage. He joined the research and consultancy group Comedia in 1994, after 15 years working in local arts development. Since then, he has been particularly concerned with the impact of cultural activity, including new approaches to evaluation, and the place of culture in democratic societies. He has undertaken work for transnational and national bodies, local authorities, foundations and cultural organisations throughout Europe, in north and south America, Africa and Japan. His work has been widely published and translated.

Sue Millar is Director of the Centre for Cultural and Heritage Management, University of Greenwich. She has alternated the two professions of museum educator and university academic specialising in cultural and heritage management. In the 1970s she was in charge of education at the Geffrye Museum, moving on to the London Museum, and returning to museum education when she was appointed Head of Education and Interpretation at the National Maritime Museum, London, in 1990.

As a Senior Lecturer in History, St Mary's College, Strawberry Hill, between 1976 and 1986, she explored the use of heritage resources in history teaching and developed the Diploma in Heritage Interpretation. At the Ironbridge Institute, University of Birmingham, between 1986 and 1990, she went on to develop the first MA in Heritage Management in Europe. Her appointment as Director of the University of Greenwich Business School in 1994 provided further opportunities for developing vocational programmes including MAs in Museum, Arts, Heritage and Cultural Tourism Management and an MBA for Small and Medium-sized Enterprises.

Millar is a trustee of the Museum of Kent Life, Cobtree, a member of the Maritime Greenwich World Heritage Site Steering Committee and a member of the Cultural Heritage National Training Organisation programme validation panel. She has been appointed a member of the Heritage Lottery Fund London Committee from 1 April 2001.

Charles Saumarez Smith was born in 1954, educated at Marlborough and King's College, Cambridge, and was a Henry Fellow at Harvard University. After studying for a doctorate at the Warburg Institute, he was appointed Christie's Research Fellow in the History of the Applied Arts at Christ's College, Cambridge. In 1982, he joined the staff of the Victoria and Albert Museum as an Assistant Keeper with special responsibility for the Victoria and Albert/Royal College of Art MA course in the history of design, and in 1990 was appointed Head of Research. Since 1994, he has been

Director of the National Portrait Gallery. He has published widely on the history of museums and in 2002 will be Slade Professor at the University of Oxford.

Ian Walker has worked in museums since 1994. He worked in the display and curatorial departments at the London Transport Museum (now London's Transport Museum) and between 1997 and 1999 he completed the Museum Studies MA at UCL. In February of this year he left the Transport Museum to became Deputy Curator at Horsham Musuem in Sussex. He has helped organise two previous events for the Institute of Ideas. In 1999 at the Culture Wars conference he organised a session debating whether museums are 'dumbing down'. Last year he helped to organise a conference at the British Museum.

Museums for 'The People'?

Josie Appleton

'The position [on culture] staked out by some conservatives, which has changed little over time, speaks for itself; they sanction fortifying the dykes. The position staked out by liberals and leftists, which has changed, raises questions. Once upon a time they believed in a new and better culture for people. No longer. In the name of democracy they anoint the daily fare of entertainment and movies; their confidence in a transformed future has evaporated... They ratify the status quo in the name of democracy.'

Russell Jacoby, **The End of Utopia** [1]

'Plenty of people will try to give the masses, as they call them, an intellectual food prepared and adapted in the way they think proper for the actual condition of the masses.'

Matthew Arnold, **Culture and Anarchy** [2]

1: INTRODUCTION

Last year, during the screening of the TV programme *Big Brother*, an exhibition was built around the show in the newly opened Wellcome Wing of the Science Museum. The exhibition posed questions such as whether or not the contestants would be harmed by their experiences, then asked visitors: 'would you like to be a guinea pig in the Big Brother house?' Three options were given, Yes/No/Don't know. Votes were clocked up in large electronic numbers. Upstairs on the floor 'Who am I?' visitors could explore the principles of genetic fingerprinting on a mock fruit-machine, matching up the DNA bands of father, mother and offspring. On the floor 'Digitopolis' they could create digital music or set up their own website. The wing was semi-dark, bathed in spacey sounds and moving lights. Here was a museum: but not as we know it.

An interview with one of the Wellcome Wing project leaders, Heather Mayfield, illustrates the thrust behind the project. When some of the interactive machines broke down, Mayfield's direct telephone number was flashed up 'for all those dissatisfied visitors' [3]. The focus of the wing seems less to produce exhibitions with high-quality scientific or intellectual content, than to attract and engage its visitors. The exhibitions on the ground floor of the Wellcome Wing change frequently, according to whatever the curators think will excite interest at the time. Many of the interactive machines ask visitors what they think about current scientific controversies, such as the use of drugs to treat depression, foot-and-mouth disease, or the male pill. The museum is anxious to assure its visitors that their views are important and will be taken very seriously by scientists, though what happens to all the Yesses/Noes/Don't knows is not clear.

The Wellcome Wing is not alone. In recent years, a new generation of museum professionals, backed by the New Labour government, has begun to create a new type of museum. In this people-centred museum, the visitor has become the focus of the museum's activity: everything, from the physical layout to the choice of exhibition to the organisation of the collection is assessed in terms of how it will appeal to and stimulate people. Like politicians and media moguls, museum officials also love The People, so much so, that the original purpose of museums, the collection, study and exhibition of objects, is now subordinate to a vast array of other social activities.

Turning museums towards The People in this way is not just a change of direction or an embellishment of what went before. It is a total reversal of the meaning and purpose of the museum and puts in question the existence of museums as such. For 200 years, from the creation of the Louvre by the French republican government as the first national museum open to the general public, the central concern of

curators was the collection, preservation and study of objects deemed to be of artistic, historic or scientific interest. The museum was organised around its collections. Because these collections were held in perpetuity on behalf of the public, museums have always had a concern with, and sense of obligation to, society at large. Whatever the ideological bent of those who ran the museum, the fact that it was bound by a clearly defined professional obligation gave its activity some rational purpose. The new museum, by contrast, organised around the ever-changing presumed needs of people, lacks any rational foundation whatsoever. Its function bends and twists to fit perceived demands, most of which are arbitrarily chosen by the government or the museum authorities themselves, and which often have no connection with the original core activity of the museum.

We can identify two key trends which have led to this state of affairs. These trends can be summarised briefly as the ascendancy over a period of 20-30 years of two seemingly opposed, yet ultimately compatible ideologies: the ideology of the economic right on the one side, and of the cultural left on the other.

Cultural leftism has gained supremacy in academic and intellectual circles since the 1960s. The enduring legacy of the cultural left has been its hostility to the idea of objectivity itself. For the cultural left, the claim to objective knowledge was no more than an attempt by the establishment to assert its intellectual hegemony. Expressed in various forms – postcolonial and feminist theories, post-modernism, Foucauldian theories of power relations – the cultural left undermined every attempt at objective truth and universality. Foucauldian theories had an especially pernicious influence within the museum profession: the acts of collecting, categorising and interpreting objects came to be seen not as the disinterested pursuit of knowledge, but as the striving for power on the part of the Western elite. The very act of building collections was seen as an affirmation of Western racism and imperialism. Collections were deemed no longer to have any meaning distinct from the subjective interpretations imposed on them by scholars and curators. The result was a loosening of the bonds which tied the scholar and curator to their objects. If all interpretations were subjective, then why privilege the one which laid false claims to objectivity? Freed from the discipline of objective knowledge, those in museums now had unprecedented scope for the exercise of whim and fancy.

The intellectual nihilism of the cultural left was compounded by the attack on traditional institutions from the economic right. Under the Conservative government of Margaret Thatcher, public arts bodies were forced to justify their existence by proving that they could give value for money. Under the new market criteria, arts bodies became service delivery organisations. 'The customer always comes first' was the new mantra. If the arts could not find customers, then they would have to go to the wall. Having lost their intellectual bearings, museum professionals were now pushed decisively in a new direction – towards the new market ideology of customer satisfaction. At the same time, they could justify this move in pseudo-democratic terms: 'The People have been excluded from museums for too long

– time to give them a say in what we do'. Thatcherism saved the cultural left by giving a focus and a rationale to its activities: having lost the rigour he once found in his professional work, the museum official could now fall back on one overriding criterion of judgement, 'does the customer like it?' The peculiar mixture of economic rightism and cultural leftism explains the odd jargon of the new official. He speaks with a leftish social conscience (The People, social inclusion, accessibility, raising self-esteem), but delivers all these as services which can be measured, audited and justified in hard-nosed market terms (such as 'benchmarking', 'best value' and so on). Just as the New Economy business speaks of meeting the diverse needs of its customers, so the new museum speaks of meeting the diverse needs of The People.

This coming together of two seemingly opposed forces reached its triumphant apogee in the election of the New Labour government in 1997. For the first time, the state, big business and culture all spoke the same language – empowerment, inclusiveness, diversity and customer satisfaction. The new orthodoxy was churned out from the new super-ministry at the Department for Culture, Media and Sport (DCMS).

Most new museum professionals have grasped this moment with enthusiasm. No longer simple curators or scholars, now they are social campaigners, out there on the frontline, fighting for The People, raising health/ environmental/gender/identity awareness. The heady effects of the new orthodoxy can be seen throughout the profession. David Fleming, director of Tyne and Wear museums and convenor for Group for Large Local Authority Museums (GLLAM), told the 2000 Museums Association conference: 'I came into museums because it was my way of trying to change the world'. An admirable aim, of course, but maybe Fleming should have become a politician or a social worker rather than a museum director.

A GLLAM report on museums and social inclusion [4] offers some examples of museums which now function as composite health, education and social service centres. An Asian women's textile project at the Birmingham Museum and Art Gallery is run in collaboration with social services and targets isolated Asian women with mental health problems. Describing the benefits of the project, the report states: 'Not only does this project enable the women to improve their skills and self-confidence, but it also provides a safe space for mental health issues to be confronted and discussed'. Tyne and Wear Museum worked with Michael - 'a real tearaway [who] became involved in the production of a CD-ROM for the museum, and gained enormously in self-esteem'. Once museums are freed from the core obligation to their collections there are almost no limits to their functions.

As their functions become more loose and wide-ranging, so the sense of their own importance becomes more grandiose. The Museums Association draft code of ethics, 'Museums for People'[5], lists in its obligatory mission statement 'key museum values', all of which, we are told, are founded on the 'expectations of the public'. (How the Museums Association worked out the public's expectations is not made clear). Each section begins with the clause 'Society expects that museums will...'. Instead of simply saying, 'Museums will do such and such', the Museums Association constitutes itself as Society, then proceeds to submit to the demands of its alter ego.

Museums, which once concentrated on organising and classifying objects, now, with the active encouragement of government, are much more interested in classifying, segmenting and categorising the public. The visitor is always treated as a group-member, never as an individual. Artefacts are no longer seen to have universal appeal, but are divided up on the basis of the particular social group to which they are deemed to be of interest. Exhibitions on African art or slavery are seen to be of interest to black British communities; the Science Museum constructed an exhibition on sport to appeal to teenage boys.

Museums vie with each other in drawing in the key target groups: the young, ethnic minorities and the economically marginalised. The DCMS suggests that museums identify an excluded group and their 'distribution', then 'engage them and establish their needs' [6]. In keeping with the new market-driven spirit, all museums funded by the DCMS now have to publish access targets and detail measures by which they are 'widening access to a broad cross-section of the public for example by age, social class, and ethnicity' [7]. Museum exhibitions, it suggests, should consciously attempt to appeal to the young as well as the old, Asian as well as white, working class as well as middle class. The diverse needs of all these different groups of people should be at the forefront of curators' minds, and inform every aspect of their work.

2: GOOD FOR THE COLLECTION?
A: THE COLLECTION IN DECLINE

Once a museum puts the perceived needs of the people at the heart of its work, the collection will quite naturally lose its importance and value. A collection is no longer seen as valuable in itself – because it is rare or beautiful, or because it represents something important within a particular field. Instead, its value is embodied in something external to itself: the immediate relationship it is able to establish to the public, how it will help the museum and its officials connect with the public, or how it will lead to observable changes in the lives of visitors.

The loss of collections' value can be observed in many aspects of museum practice. Sometimes collections are left to gather dust while museums get on with more exciting and socially responsible activities. In the GLLAM case studies of best practice, museum projects involved awareness-raising about teenage pregnancy, or setting up a football team with young vandals. The report argues that a reorientation towards social ends will show why collections 'are worth having in the first place'. But in practice the desired social ends are more easily achieved without bringing artefacts into it. If they are used, the objects become no more than props for the wider social project to which they have no necessary connection.

Sometimes interactive exhibits replace objects. If the main concern of a museum is to engage the public in particular ways, these aims might be better achieved with animation or interactive technologies than with the raw object. The simple object allows for an open encounter with no predetermined outcome – the visitor can make of it what he likes. Interactive technology only allows for closed outcomes because the encounter is all programmed in advance by the museum. For museums geared towards building relationships with the people, an open-ended encounter between visitor and object leaves far too much to chance. Likewise, animated contraptions, which sometimes replace original specimens, are calculated to elicit a desired effect. The animated tyrannosaurus rex at the Natural History Museum, for example, elicits the 'Wow, scary' effect. In the most extreme cases, collections can be broken up and dispersed. The new Commission for Museums Libraries and Archives put forward the argument that accessibility would be increased by 'deaccessioning' collections, ie, dispersing parts of them to targeted community centres that a museum may deem to be particularly worthy recipients. Paradoxically, the effect of such measures would be to make collections accessible only to those communities chosen by the museum, while making them increasingly inaccessible to the population as a whole.

Forming links with specific communities is taken to its logical extreme by simply giving objects back. Influenced by similar cases in the USA, Glasgow Museums repatriated the Lakota Ghost Dance Shirt to a tribe of Native Americans. Mark O'Neill, of Glasgow Museums, told a Museums and Galleries Commission conference in 2000 that the loss of the shirt was outweighed by the benefits of 'bringing healing to a sad people'. Unusual as this case is (there has been much talk of restitution, but little action, so far), it nevertheless reveals an important shift. Some museum professionals seem to value the demonstration of empathy and social responsibility more highly than they value the collections they are supposed to protect.

Increasingly, the aim of exhibitions seems aimed more at drawing in a particular audience, by creating a deliberate shock effect. In the summer of 2000, the Victoria and Albert Museum (V&A) staged an exhibition of modern design by Ron Arad next to medieval religious icons. Curator Susan Lambert told me that the exhibition was 'going for a slightly different audience' that was not 'on top of Christian symbolism'. She 'wanted a visual spectacle', that would get new people looking at old objects.

B: CURATORS AND SCHOLARSHIP

Advocates of the people-centred museum argue that collections have no intrinsic value anyway. Their value lies instead in their relationship to The People. At best, this is a statement of the obvious. Without society, without thought and knowledge, there would be no museums and objects would have no value in any meaningful sense of the word. It is true also, that society's understanding and appreciation of objects changes through time. Charles Saumarez Smith has traced the V&A's treatment of the Mark Lane doorway, which started out as the carved wooden front for a late seventeenth century London house. In the late nineteenth century it was acquired by the museum for the quality of its woodwork, and in the late twentieth century was placed in the V&A shop. As time passed, the same object was seen by turns to have a decorative, historical, aesthetic and commercial value [8].

However, just because different societies might bring to light different or even conflicting aspects of the same object does not mean that the aesthetic or scientific value of those objects is arbitrary. Society might impose its tastes upon museum collections – classifying, organising and interpreting in its own way. But that is only one side of the relationship, because objects also impose themselves upon society. The Parthenon marbles did not gain their importance from the whim of Lord Elgin or the British Museum. They hold their exalted place today because of their artistic greatness, the perfection of the craftsmanship and their unique historical significance in relation both to the art of Periclean Athens and to the entire Western tradition.

It is the task of scholarship to assess the relative importance of objects, for what they are in themselves and for the broader artistic, scientific or historical context within which they are to be placed. Collections are evidence – of past societies, of different cultures, species of bird, forms of rock, etc. Collections are the raw material of our knowledge on so many subjects. The study of works of art develops our ideas about art as such, just as the study of the products of nature develops our ideas about the natural world, or the study of the artefacts of past societies develops our ideas about history. Knowledge is not some arbitrary ideological construct within our minds. In the specific context of museums, knowledge comes from the critical encounter between the scholar and his raw material.

It is rare for the core activities of curatorship and scholarship to be done away with altogether. Instead, they are swamped by an ever-expanding array of 'audience-related' activities. In the last 30 years there has been a remorseless growth in education, helpdesk and marketing functions. A survey on museum research and scholarship documented the sense among many curators that their research function was under threat [9]. 80 percent said that they were not as active in research as they would like to be, and most said the time available for research had declined in the past ten years. However even these figures do not fully convey the depth of the malaise. Much of what now passes for research would have been done in the past by the marketing department (if there even was one). Many curators now spend an increasing amount of their time researching the public and the attitudes of the public towards their work.

Often a museum's small numbers of curators are expected to double up as PR officers and managers. In London's Science Museum scientists are asked to go to the galleries to talk to the public about their work. The aim of these sessions seems less to help the public understand science, than to help curators build relationships with their visitors (or to pretend to include the public in the process of making science). Many museums emphasise the importance of management training – the Cultural Heritage National Training Organisation now produces courses in management for museum professionals.

Fewer people entering the museum profession today have the specialist training necessary to study and care for collections. Many enter the profession, not by gaining a doctorate in art history or palaeontology, for example, but by doing a one-year Museums Studies MA (this is especially the case for those working in local and independent museums).

A small proportion of the Museums Studies course is concerned with the conservation and interpretation of artefacts – most is concerned with the study of audiences and cultural theory analyses of power in exhibitions. In response to this training gap, University College London has created a separate Artefact Studies MA. Expertise in objects, it seems, is just one of the many functions of the new curator. Even when curators have studied their collections, they are often asked to defer to non-specialists when organising exhibitions – administrators, PR officers, or members of the public themselves. Tyne and Wear museum has encouraged the display of works which 'may not necessarily be famous or highly regarded, but instead have been chosen by members of the public simply because they like them or because they arouse certain emotions or memories'. [10]

Underlying all these changes is the declining authority of scholarship itself. The advance of cultural relativism throughout the Western academic system had already shattered the belief among scholars that there was anything intrinsically valuable held by museums, or that their understanding of objects was any more valuable than anybody else's. Now, the elevation of the emotional well-being of the visitor put scholars further on the defensive, making them feel guilty that they would value dead objects over living people.

For scholarship to flourish, scholars must be allowed some degree of separation from the immediate demands of politicians, bureaucrats, and even from the public. They must be allowed to study their subject and to follow the demands of their own discipline without having to wonder all the time whether it is directly relevant to the public. The question of how to communicate the results of their research to the public will come at the stage of creating exhibitions. But in the process of original research, intellectual concentration necessarily means the exclusion of concerns external to the matter in hand. If scholars are forced to listen to the clamour of discordant voices outside their profession, the chances of profound insights are slim indeed.

If scholarship in museums is neglected, our knowledge will suffer. Museums cannot simply rest on the expertise they have built up over the years. There must be a constant replenishment of that knowledge by scholars who keep up with the latest research and who are ready always to reassess the significance and meaning of objects. If this central task falls into neglect, it will be very difficult to repair the damage done. If, for example, the expert in fossil reptiles has been redeployed to study how people react to fossil reptiles, he is less likely to concentrate on new discoveries in the field. At worst, whole branches of knowledge could go into decline through wilful neglect.

C: THE SOCIALLY RESPONSIBLE MUSEUM

While the core function for which museums were created is downgraded to an ancillary activity, a vast range of spurious functions are loaded on to them for which they are entirely unsuited. For the new orthodoxy, museums must reflect the concerns and experiences of our society and of everyday life. They must become relevant, and inclusive, and should talk to 'real people'. Sociology professor Tony Bennett complains that nineteenth century museums were exclusive, as they showed no interest in the lives and habits of working people [11]. He praises the People's Palace in Glasgow for talking to real living people because it allows them to recognise themselves in public life. Most museums offer something similar to Tyne and Wear's commitment 'to try to reflect and involve the whole community in its exhibitions and activities' [12].

Museums try to make themselves relevant in two different ways. The first method is to cling to the appeal of mass entertainment. The logic here is crude, but occasionally effective: lots of people watch TV (for example); therefore museums should use TV in their exhibition to pull in the crowds. Exhibitions based around this principle include the museum for popular music in Sheffield, the Brand.new exhibition at the V&A and the video games in the Wellcome Wing. The second approach is to target specific groups, such as women, youth, or ethnic minorities. This strategy is far less effective because it almost always involves some massive presumption on the part of the museum as to what appeals to these groups.

Social inclusion is another crusade aimed at transforming the function of the museum. In the improbable circumstances of his 1999 budget speech, chancellor Gordon Brown committed museums to the struggle against social exclusion [13]. The DCMS had the vision of museums becoming 'centres for social change', improving people's self-esteem and improving community relations, while the GLLAM social inclusion report defined seven social ends to which museums should gear themselves, such as personal growth and development, community empowerment and tackling unemployment and crime.

More widespread concerns about social cohesion and the decline of the traditional bonds of church, family and political parties have led commentators to search for alternative sources of social bonding. This concern was no doubt heightened by the apathy implied by the historically low turnout in the recent general election. Museums are seen as 'cultural meeting places' that could fill the gaps left by the decline of the old institutions and bring cohesion to a fragmented society. New Labour thinkers Charles Leadbeater and Kate Oakley write that 'art, culture and sport create meeting places for people in an increasingly diversified, fragmented and unequal society', meeting places that were once 'provided by work, religion or trade unions' [14]. This explains the interest with which government watched the crowds bustling at Tate Modern.

There is nothing new about using museums and cultural institutions for social purposes. In the early nineteenth century Prime Minister Sir Robert Peel stated that one of the purposes of the new National Gallery would be to 'cement the bonds of union between the richer and poorer orders of the state' [15]. Such a sentiment would chime with those of our present cultural elite. The crucial qualification, however, was that the National Gallery would give access to great works of art. Museums can be used for all sorts of purposes, some good, some bad. Conveying the insights of art and science is a mighty social task. Using art and science to prop up the existing ruling caste is a less glorious cause. But as long as the core functions of the museum – the preservation, study and display of collections – are not interfered with and retain their central role, the added contribution of politicians and bureaucrats can be dispensed with by the visitor.

In the people-centred museum, however, social ends tend to take over. Much of the activity of museum staff is now indistinguishable from that of a host of social, health or educational services. Most of the DCMS or GLLAM case-studies of best social inclusion practice could have been performed by any charity or social service. The collection and the specialist knowledge required to understand it are pushed to the margins. In its efforts to provide every sort of service, from health to social support, the people-centred museum tends to undermine the distinctive character and eventually the very rationale of the museum as such. This is compounded by efforts to dissolve the museum into its community, to break down any barriers with the world around. Outreach programmes, attempts to involve local communities in the museum's activities, and the outright dispersal of the collection into community centres; all these blur the museum out of existence. When the newly appointed head of Re:source Matthew Evans suggested in February 2000 that museums get away from the idea that they are constrained by physical walls and that they should get their collections into shops, clubs and pubs, many in the profession reacted at first with surprise. 'We're already there, we're doing it', said Simon Thurley, director of the Museum of London.

A good museum will give the visitor the opportunity to withdraw from the mundane cares and concerns of everyday life and to contemplate instead something which may be remote from his own experience. A good museum will of necessity be different and separate from the world, not because it deliberately and pretentiously sets out to be different, but because its contents (one hopes) will not be everyday things. On the other hand, a museum that tries only to replicate the world around and dissolve itself into it, has lost both its reason and its will to exist.

3: GOOD FOR THE PEOPLE?

Advocates of the new museum say that because museums are public institutions funded by public money, they must answer to all the people and not just to a cultural elite. This seems a reasonable argument. So let us examine how well the people-centred museum fulfils its obligations. Perhaps a categorical distinction might guide us here. The distinction is between 'The People' as imagined by the museum profession, and the older concept of the public. The public forms itself, independently of any guiding authority from above, such as the state. It is an amorphous and ill-defined entity, typically made up of abstract individuals. The People, on the other hand, is formed by the state or one of its institutions. It is a projection on the part of those in authority on to those over whom it has authority, an attempt to define, classify and categorise according to its own needs. Joe Public does not exist among The People. He is far too vague an individual. The People is made up of many different categories of people, all well defined (by the state). Diversity is the great buzzword among supporters of The People. Because of the talk about diversity and difference, it appears more individualistic. But this individual does not make

himself, he is always created from above, by authority.

In the case of the new museum, The People that they are so anxious to follow are a pure projection, a creation by the museums themselves. Nobody outside the cultural elite ever demanded that museums become more accessible, relevant, inclusive, diverse and interactive. All these views were hatched within government and the museums world itself and then projected out on to the public.

The consequences of orienting the museum towards The People are two-fold. As the Dome proved beyond doubt, when the new cultural elite start second-guessing what people want, they invariably underestimate them and try to go for the lowest common denominator. Reaching for the lowest common denominator explains the growing tendency in museums to treat all visitors as children. It is strange how, for all the talk of different needs, the child tends to provide the universal model for the public. Secondly, the people focus also leads museums to build manipulative and invasive relationships with their visitors. When the purpose of an exhibition lies in its relationship to the visitor, the museum will, quite naturally, want to check to see if the relationship is working. People become the objects of study, their interests and responses catalogued and catered to. In the new museum the observation of the masses has replaced the study of things.

Direct address and forced chumminess are favoured to assist the visitor; impersonal and abstract terms are now considered too cold and too user-unfriendly. Both the Science Museum and the Natural History Museum use the second person in their exhibitions on human biology: 'This is your brain', 'Have you ever wondered where your relatives came from?', as if people would not be interested if the model was of the human brain, in the abstract. At a Natural History Museum exhibit on leaf structure and function, a voiceover announces: 'Welcome to the leaf factory. You are an 8,000th of your normal size and are inside the leaf.' An intellectual regression seems to be taking place here. Making the abstraction from the particular 'me' to the general human is not only fundamental to thought itself, but is something that children grasp at school. This shift in style of presentation, trivial as it is, is still very revealing. On a visit to the High Street Londinium exhibition in the Museum of London, I overheard the following exchange between a member of staff dressed in a toga and a visitor:

Actress: 'My husband has gone to the amphitheatre. Come in and help yourself to food. There's some nice cheese over there...'

Visitor: 'How do you know they made cheese?'

Actress: 'What do you mean *they*? This is me you're talking about'.

'Me', 'you', not 'they'. Don't question, don't try to stand back, says the new museum.

The new museum aims to help people understand through fabricated feelings and experience rather than by reason. Full-scale reconstructions such as the Jorvik Viking Centre and High Street Londinium at the Museum of London are presented with the claim that visitors gain an authentic experience of the past. 'Visit the Jorvik Viking Centre, step aboard a time car and be whisked back through the centuries to real-life Viking Britain... You can experience in sight, sound and smell exactly what it was like to live and work in Viking-age Jorvik'. 'Leave year 2000, and enter High Street Londinium, first century AD... You enter Londinium early in the morning'. Both of these reconstructions are based on actual archaeological digs; they are representations and interpretations of the evidence uncovered. Why does this evidence need to be presented as a 'real' picture of the past, rather than what it is, archaeological evidence? Any opportunity for the visitor to exercise his imagination is severely curtailed.

At the Museum of Verulamium in St Albans a complete Roman skeleton lies in a battered but elaborate lead coffin. From tooth-wear studies we know that he ate high-quality soft foods, and the style of his coffin suggests a high social class. His face can be reconstructed from skull shape and from the calcification of his skeleton we can guess his age. Twenty years ago, the solution would probably have been to present this information next to the skeleton, leaving visitors to make their own image of the man. So much of the fascination of this exhibit is that we do not know what this man was like. Unfortunately, today's visitors cannot be left alone to make these imaginative leaps. A video next to the skeleton conjures up the man. The dark shadow of the past is transformed into an upper-middle-class man poncing around the streets of St Albans in a toga, narrating the story of his life and death: 'My coffin, as befits my status, had the highest quality detail!'

Many museums seem to think the public has the most limited capacity for concentration and little need for quiet. The proliferation of gadgets and interactive displays, flashing lights, talking exhibits, music and sound effects tells us more about museums' view of the public than it does about the public itself. Children have limited concentration and are still at the stage of 'learning through play'. But adults can read books for hours on end; they can sit and concentrate on ideas without moving their body, without playing or physically engaging in any way. Indeed, concentration in stillness is the only way most adults can think in a sustained manner.

A common refrain from the new museums and their government backers is that many of the visitors they want to attract are from marginalised social groups and are therefore easily intimidated – a patronising and rather strange perception of the public. One of the 'barriers to access' identified by the DCMS is 'attitudinal', that is 'museums not making all of their visitors feel welcomed and valued' [16]. To draw in the shy masses, museums now create spaces for public participation. In order to bolster people's confidence, some museums - such as the Tyne and Wear Museum and the People's Gallery in Birmingham – show community exhibitions chosen and curated by local people. Other museums help their visitors to feel valued by asking their opinion in the exhibition, such as the 'Tell us what you think' exhibits in the Science Museum's Wellcome Wing.

Museums were once places where individuals could go in and be left alone to reflect on something that had nothing to do with their everyday lives. Now, in their every move the public are watched and examined, giving the relationship of museums to their public a predatory aspect – museums feed off the shifting source of public opinion and reaction.

Officials debate how architecture affects the way visitors move around buildings. Questionnaires and focus groups analyse visitor response to exhibits, or their understanding of a particular label. Visitor figures are monitored to see what ethnic group, what age or gender group is underrepresented and the missing groups can then be targeted.

While making few intellectual demands, exhibitions set up to engage visitors can be very demanding in other ways. People are not left to wander through the museum with their own thoughts, looking at an object or reading a label as they choose. To obtain information visitors often must press a button. This seems less a means to an end than an end in itself – the temperature and pressure of the planets of the solar system, for example, could be printed on a card, yet the Natural History Museum has interactive exhibits that provide these basic facts. Action is often demanded just to see an object. In the Jersey Maritime Museum some of the text accompanying exhibits is hidden away in models of shells, boats and bottles that the visitor must open up if they wish to see it.

We arrive then at a paradox. The curator who is concerned with The People, who loudly professes his respect for every ethnic, class, age and gender group and who builds his exhibition around what he perceives to be their needs, almost inevitably ends up expressing disdain for the public. On the other hand, the curator who is concerned above all with his collection, is more truly respectful towards the public. In his fidelity to his own work, he assumes that visitors are intelligent enough to understand what he has done and to appreciate the effort he has invested. 'The People's' curator is motivated (or is proclaimed so) by a concern not to look down on people, but ends up doing just that. The objects' curator starts with an unabashed belief in the superiority of expertise, but nevertheless treats all as equals.

In the new museum, the honest scholar, the curator with a genuine love for his subject is pushed to the margins, or might be redesignated as a helpdesk assistant. In his place comes the service delivery manager with his social conscience on permanent display. For this type of person, the visitors are his subjects, in every sense of the word.

4: CONCLUSION

Museums should stick to what they do best – to preserve, display, study and where possible collect the treasures of civilisation and of nature. They are not fit to do anything else. It is this single rationale for the museum that makes each one unique, which gives each its own distinctive character. It is the hard work of scholars and curators in their own areas of expertise that attracts visitors. Everybody knows that the harder you try to win friends and ingratiate yourself with people, the more you repel them. It would seem however that those running our new museums need to learn afresh this simple human lesson.

[1] Russell Jacoby, *The End Of Utopia*, Basic Books, 1999

[2] Matthew Arnold, *Culture and Anarchy*, Yale University Press, 1994

[3] *Museums Journal*, September 2000

[4] GLLAM, October 2000, *Museums and Social Inclusion*

[5] Museums Association, Draft code of Ethics, *Museums for People*, October 2000

[6] DCMS, *Centres for social change: museums, galleries and archives for all*, 2000

[7] DCMS, *Museums for the many*, 1999

[8] Saumarez Smith, Charles, 'Museums, artefacts and meanings', in Peter Vergo, *The New Museology*, Reaktion Books, 1989

[9] Gunn, Ann V and Prescott, RGW, *Lifting the Veil: Research and Scholarship in United Kingdom Museums and Galleries*, 1999

[10] DCMS, *Museums for the many*, 1999

[11] Lumley, Robert, *The Museum Time Machine: putting cultures on display*, 1988

[12] DCMS, *Museums for the many*, 1999

[13] The Social Exclusion Unit defines social exclusion as 'what can happen when people or areas suffer from a combination of linked problems such as unemployment, poor skills, low incomes, poor housing, high crime environments' DCMS, *Centres for Social Change: Museums, Galleries and Archives for all*, 2000

[14] Leadbeater, Charles and Oakley, Kate, *The Independents*, Demos, 1999

[15] Cited in Richard Sandell, *Museums as Agents of Inclusion* in Museum and Management Curatorship 17 (4), 1998

[16] DCMS, *Museums for the many*, 1999

The death of the curator

Sue Millar

*'Now three of the museums with the most comprehensive
collections of modern art – MoMA in New York, The Musee
National d'Art Moderne at the Pompidou Centre in Paris
and the new Tate Modern in London – are rethinking the
ways in which they tell the story of the twentieth century.
…In London, the new Tate will essay a …radical approach,
adopting four broad thematic groupings, each covering a
whole century and juxtaposing contemporary and
historical works, so that the visitor is constantly reminded
that we view the past through the frame of the present.*

*The increasing complexity and sophistication of such
presentations will make the viewer even more conscious
that it is the mind and eye of the curator which shape the
display of a collection, while allowing a new freedom for
the spectator to select his or her own path through the
century'.*

Nicholas Serota, **Experience or Interpretation, The Dilemma
of Museums of Modern Art**, 2000

The Director of the Tate Gallery, Sir Nicholas Serota, takes a
calm, rational, balanced approach to the question of
displaying modern works of art. In his vision the curator
plays a pivotal role in stimulating readings of the collection
and creating the conditions in which visitors can experience
a sense of discovery for themselves. In attempting to
redress and refute many of the neatly crafted, polemical
statements made by Josie Appleton, with the realities of the
museum business I have begun with an icon.

The Tate Gallery at Bankside, London – a former power
station and dramatic landmark – has been a remarkable
success story since it opened a year ago. Visitor figures
have outstripped all expectations. As an archetypal modern
museum Tate Modern combines urban regeneration tool,
tourist attraction, commercial activities, public social
space, educational resource and community asset with
consummate ease. The adaptive re-use of the building and
the interpretation of the collections are intellectually brave
without being condescending or intimidating to the public.
Moreover, the members of staff I spoke to in the cloakroom
and café, all drawn from the locality, are enthusiastic and
proud to work in such an exciting place. They like the

atmosphere. Unwittingly, they probably also contribute to the statistics for the employment of local labour, particularly young people from ethnic minority backgrounds.

The people versus objects debate is a false dichotomy. The government gave a simple definition of museums in a statement from the Department of Culture, Media and Sport, (24 July 1998): 'Museums are about objects and for people'. It is true that in many smaller, local authority and independent museums a few individuals are struggling to fulfil multiple roles. But the notion that we should return to a supposedly utopian era when curators were free to pursue so-called 'objective' scholarship irrespective of external political pressures as a blueprint for the twenty-first century is retrograde in the extreme.

There were, and still are, good scholar/curators. 20 to 30 years ago, however, a large number of curators could be regarded as 'object-oriented hobbyists'. They pursued their own lines of enquiry in a vacuum, using their specialist expertise to advise on sale-room authenticity, adding to the collections in a haphazard manner, successfully ignoring the rigours and tedium of cataloguing, providing limited displays and avoiding contact with the public. The result of a reluctance to engage in political debate or promote the significance of museums in reflecting and interpreting the values of the places they served has been the overall diminution of the place of museums within local authority hierarchies. Museums have lost out in leisure and cultural services departments during a period of unprecedented expansion in the sector overall. Curatorial malaise has been a major contributory factor. Only two museum

directors are chief officers.

The British Museum, like other national museums and galleries, still employs curators in traditional roles. Currently, there is a funding crisis. The entrenched and old-fashioned views prevalent at the Museum led the Managing Director, Suzanna Taverne, to hand in her resignation in September 2001. 'There is a priesthood of curators, who look after the relics. There's this notion that only they can be the intermediaries between the relics and the public. They carry this sacred flame of the institution – the museum' (The Sunday Times, 9 September 2001). She considers the Museum places too much emphasis on curatorial expertise at the expense of management skills. One 'twentysomething' couple I spoke to recently agreed. Following a visit to the British Museum they contrasted the mismatch between the 'boring temporary exhibition' they had just seen and the breathtaking vistas of the Norman Foster Great Court and accompanying professionally mounted exhibition promoting his architectural practice.

I argue here – as I have done elsewhere – that the role of the curator is changing or disappearing altogether and that this is the right way forward for museums. The art curator is often peripatetic – travelling from one continent to another curating exhibitions, researching and publishing widely. These individuals are the highly trained specialists often with doctoral qualifications. This type of curatorship role is rightly flourishing. Such a definition of curatorship is distinct from the permanent scholarly 'lifetime' appointments at the British Museum. It is also different from a curatorial role that envisages the curator running a small or medium sized museum combining scholarship and management – looking after access, education and exhibition programmes as well as caring for and developing the collection.

It is this 'Jack/Jill of all trades' type of curatorial role that is rapidly disappearing. A range of specialisms (conservator, educator, manager, researcher, information systems' officer, collections manager, visitor services manager, designer etc) is emerging to replace the one individual. In essence the curator has become a manager/director in function if not in name. She or he will appoint a range of paid staff, contract staff and volunteers to support the delivery of individual projects and programmes. The scope for partnerships and alliances is starting to be recognised and exploited in a changing context for museums and curatorship. Maritime museums have a purchasing consortium. University academics and curators work together to undertake research projects at the Natural History Museum in London and Manchester University Museum. There are an increasing number of links between archive, library and museums collections, by virtue of the formation of Re:source, the Council for Museums, Archives and Libraries. Re:source views collections as valuable resources. Displays in public houses are not an outrageous suggestion but the proposal has been a headline stopper. The national collection's reservoir is full of interesting and intrinsically valuable two and three-dimensional artefacts. Outreach displays are not an 'either' 'or' option but a question of seeking out additional audiences on their own patch with storage solved into the bargain.

I suggest the role of the curator, as we have known it, is now dead, dying or has already changed. The new breed of museum director has to prioritise people and collections in harmonious symbiosis.

The curator's tale

Ian Walker

As a curator, there are three things that I want to say in response to Josie Appleton's essay. The first is that the importance now attributed to the audience by museums is having a significant effect on the role of the curator. Secondly, that the changing views of the curator's role are undermining both the value and the appreciation of museums. Thirdly many of the features of current museum practice that Ms Appleton cites as evidence of change for the worse, things such as marketing, interpretation and IT, are not bad in and of themselves.

Appleton is correct when she points out that there has been a huge shift in the staffing of museums over the last few years. As far as I am aware this growth has taken place in the soft 'user-focused' departments. An example would be London's Transport Museum where I worked until earlier this year. When I first started there in 1995 the education department consisted of one full time and one part time member of staff. By 2001 the department, now known as the Education and Interpretation Department, employed six people. A similar rate of growth took place in the marketing department.

In the case of the Transport Museum it means that it has a very good education service and also that it is very well marketed. Having dynamic departments of this size clearly improved and developed the museum and I expect a similar level of improvement has taken place across the museum world. While I would give a guarded welcome to the investment museums are making in education and marketing (as well as in new technologies), I do have one major concern. These initiatives rarely improve the quality of the collection or even how it is presented to the public. A marketing department might improve visitor figures, for example, by organising children's parties or special concerts. As 'creativity' moves to the centre of the curriculum, museum education departments have an almost infinite range of opportunities, even though the real usefulness of the collection to pupils might be very limited.

As those from an education or marketing background rise to more senior positions, a museum's success will tend to be measured more and more in educational and marketing terms, less and less in terms of the quality of the collection. But it is the collection which makes a museum unique. It could be a narrow special interest collection – such as the Fan Museum in Greenwich for example. It could be parochial, like many regional museums. Or it could be one of the great national collections such as the British Museum. The ascendancy of what is peripheral over what is core, what every museum does (and in fact almost every institution in the land does) over what is unique, leads to a loss of distinctiveness and a loss of expertise.

In the new museum world, the view that the collection and the curator should come first is unfashionable. Many museums pursue political agendas that have little or nothing to do with their collections. Just one recent example is a touring exhibition organised by The Petrie and Croydon Museums and the Burrell Collection. 'Digging for Dreams' was ostensibly an exhibition of Egyptian artefacts. But it also had as its goal the promotion of social and cultural inclusion in economically deprived areas. You might wonder what ancient Egypt might have to do with such a worthy cause. The curators however managed to twist a connection together: to challenge the Eurocentric portrayal of Ancient Egypt and replace it with an Afrocentric one. The idea was that black visitors would feel better about their own history, and therefore better about themselves.

It is good to take a criticial view of Egyptology as defined by the Victorian. Victorian prudery, for example, led them to ignore or gloss over the significance of onanism in Egyptian religious beliefs. However to replace this view with another partial view of the world tells us nothing about the ancient Egyptians. Moreover, unlike previous partial views, this one does not even make an attempt at an objective understanding of ancient Egypt based on the material evidence (I suspect the curators would utter a Foucauldian guffaw at the very concept).

If museum staff continue to neglect the importance of their own collections while promoting relevance, social inclusion and other political causes, museums will cease to make any unique contribution to society. Furthermore audience-focused activity will ultimately undermine the contribution to a museum that the non-curatorial staff can make. My one reservation about Josie Appleton's article is that she seems hostile to education and marketing and to things such as the use of actors, IT and interactive games. I understand and sympathise with her reservations but I would say that, when properly used, these innovations can contribute much, as they did at London's Transport Museum. But good curatorial authority must control their use. When their use is genuinely relevant to the collection, then they can serve to enhance rather than undermine it.

Extremism is the enemy

David Lowenthal

Have museums lost their soul and their métier? If so, are they uniquely deprived in our world today? At first glance, Josie Appleton's diatribe against the twin evils of economic and populist diktat is persuasive, but not because museums are uniquely threatened – far from it. The same charges should be levelled in education, the arts, and much else, and in American and European society as well as British. But on closer scrutiny Appleton's litany of ills loses credibility. Not only does she overstate her case; her own follies are as bad as those she condemns. Hardly a sentence escapes some gross generalisation, some obiter dictum, some grievous error about past or present. Extremism makes Appleton her own worst enemy.

Are the trends she deplores really 'a total reversal' of the traditional meaning and purpose of museums? Have they not always been changing? Were not museums in the past equally subject to museum authorities' whims and commands? Is the new populism only pseudo-democracy? Did artefacts ever have 'universal appeal'? Have rarity and beauty ever been the only criteria by which they have been selected for display? Is their repatriation (legally mandated internationally by UNESCO and internally by many countries)

wholly lamentable, and if so how could museums resist it? Does protecting collections really matter more than other forms of social responsibility? How many scholars' belief in their superior knowledge has been 'shattered' by cultural relativism, and how many feel guilty for valuing dead objects over living people? Would it really benefit scholars to shut out 'the clamour of discordant voices'? Does the display of everyday things, as opposed to great art, really vitiate the distinctive character of museums? If so, whose everyday things should be excised? Those of ancient Pompeii? Of medieval England? Of Victorian London?

Appleton continually asserts but never coherently explains why artefacts have an overarching value and why their care constitutes a museum's 'core function'. She admits that objects are always seen in context but falls back on their intrinsic worth as a sine qua non. Error after error flows from this assumption. She claims the Parthenon marbles 'hold their exalted place today because of their artistic greatness,' but this craftsmanship was only noted because it was brought to England and displayed, close up, to a philhellenic cognoscenti; it was only by the whim of Lord Elgin and the British Museum that they became so famous. How does their transcendant focus on 'things' make each museum unique? Appleton is so censorious toward today's museums as to make them unrecognisable. Do museums actually tend to greet all visitors as children, compel them to view specific things in specified ways, curtail the use of imagination? These are not the experiences this visitor has had, nor do they comport with most visitor responses; to the contrary, museums are widely lauded for letting visitors see what they want, for being non-directive, for letting artefacts speak for themselves. They are increasingly appreciated as user-friendly, giving the lie to Appleton's conclusion that trying to win friends and ingratiate oneself only repels people.

On both sides of the Atlantic the public has greater faith in museums than in any other purveyor of the past. In a 1995 survey, 20,000 European 15-year-olds rated museums and historic sites most reliable for understanding the past; and 1500 American interviewees declared museums and sites more trustworthy than any other source. What makes history museums so trusted? The American interviews suggest that museums and sites provide unparalleled intimacy and involvement with the past, in apparently unmediated immediacy. One visits museums and sites at one's own pace, with one's chosen companions; we are not required to look here rather than there, or constrained to any sequence; we are not told what to think but left to make up our own minds. Unlike being immured in the classroom or imbibing oldsters' tales of yore, museum-goers feel they make of the past what they themselves decide, based on seemingly objective evidence.

Museum displays also seem objective owing to their intrinsic and undeniable materiality. People trust what's in museums and sites because they see it with their own eyes; things don't lie, as is customarily said; seeing is believing. The viewer is carried back in imagination to when the bones were living creatures and the artefacts were fashioned, without the distortions that are patent in movies and television. People also trust history museums because their exhibits seem to reflect a consensus of many views, not just one, as with a schoolteacher or a textbook. The collaborative chorus of manifold voices helps make museum displays credible. As one viewer put it, 'it has been researched by more than one person [and they] all discuss things and arrive at the version' to be presented. For similar reasons, English schoolchildren gauge historical truth by citation frequency: when opinions differ, says a 13-year-old, 'look in loads of history books and the one which has the most... is the winner.' Truth is determined by a majority of experts; museums become credible by seeming to tap manifold authorities.

Homo curatorius

Richard Fortey

I confess. I am a curator. I am one of those shadowy figures in an out-of-date sports jacket and corduroy trousers who can be seen skulking in the public galleries, or slipping though locked doorways marked 'authorised personnel only'. My natural habitat is the collection. This is not the small fraction of the collection on view to the public – or should I say 'The People' following Ms Appleton? – but the hidden wealth that lies in the vaults and research rooms of a great Museum. Most of my life has been spent pursuing the kind of research which can kindly be described as esoteric, a study of fossil animals long extinct: scholarly, certainly, scientific, sometimes.

We are always being written about, us curators. We have been demonised or sanctified. We are either celebrated as the true guardians of our culture's richness, or else we are castigated as representatives of an out-of-date elitism. In tune with our sports jackets, there is still an antique image of the curator as a gentleman who eschewed trade in favour of scholarship. Now, it seems, there is a new version: 'no longer simple curators or scholars, now they are social campaigners, out there on the frontline, fighting for The People, raising health/environment/gender/identity awareness.' It is surprising how every social commentator seems to have an opinion about how the curator relates to society: usually, the curator himself (or herself) is not so confident. Instead, he will tend to disappear back into the vaults and hope that he still has a job by the end of the year after next.

Most curators I know (and I know a lot) are genuinely devoted to the collections in their care. The old title used in the national museums for the heads of the Departments is the Keeper. It is an appropriate term, because the prime responsibility will always be maintenance and guardianship of the collection. But in the better endowed museums (and there are not enough of them) there is an awareness that tending the collections for future generations is not enough: a living collection is one that is researched upon – used. Curators know that there are always discoveries to be made on their collections. Curators also know that research can be a source of pleasure and inspiration. They would be delighted to communicate to the world outside the joy of the process and the excitement of the result. But how?

First to say, we should not be prescriptive about what can or cannot comprise a collection. Many great collections of the past started out as the curious obsessions of curious people. There is nothing wrong (indeed, it's absolutely right) with collecting materials relating to social change – be it ethnic, gender, or just vernacular architectural accessories and garden gnomes. One of the best museums I visited recently was the one near the Statue of Liberty in New York, which relates the history of immigration into the United States. Thank goodness somebody curated all that ordinary stuff relating to everyday people: from bus tickets to discarded clothes. A display does not have to be a great work of art to be eloquent.

The problem lies in how and why collections are shown. Many curators don't want to spin any particular line, but they do want visitors to understand and appreciate the objects in their museum. And I really mean 'objects'. I agree with Josie Appleton that the tendency to replace real specimens with electronic games and virtual whizzbangs is short-sighted. This kind of show does not stick in the memory any more – it becomes just another TV programme. This is where conflict between the curator and the 'display professional' may arise. The former tends to view any display as an over-simplification, and demands more explanation, while the latter would send the curator back to his ivory tower with a brief nod towards his technical advice. It's not so much 'dumbing down' as 'editing out'.

We have to face the fact that it is very difficult to make a display out of the process of understanding. Allowing the general public access to the curatorial process may reveal little more than a bald, middle-aged man engrossed in piles of books and pamphlets, or with the genitalia of a pinned moth. I recently wrote a whole book about trilobites, which occupy no more than a square foot or so of display area in the Natural History Museum (much more behind the scenes, admittedly) and even so I was conscious of how much had to be left out.

Perhaps a book is the right place for this level of explanation – but it would be hard to claim that a book lacked an agenda, political or otherwise, for it would be a dull book that did not have a viewpoint. I truly don't know how much I love The People, but I do know that I very much want The People to love trilobites.

So is the public side of the museum gradually divorcing itself from the collections? Is the day of the object numbered? I hope not. In the Natural History Museum in London there are still bones of ichthyosaurs and even stuffed birds. Those who pause long enough to engage with these specimens will probably take away a memory. There have been times when the more militant of the exhibition radicals regarded these displays as indecent, even as taking up space which could better be served by electronic didacticism. I believe that the richness of the world is better served by showing the wealth of real things – animals, plants, minerals.

I've a feeling that if we replaced this reality with video games, or question-and-answer machines stressing that, 'we really care, we really do,' then the world out there – the world where the imagination should be led – will recede into the familiar cliches of the soap opera.

I believe that a reaction against such potentially politicised exhibitions is beginning. After all, the object itself is what distinguishes a museum from a TV show. As for the curator, he should prove to be the friend of the object of which he is the Keeper.

A question of taste

Maurice Davies

One of my favourite ways of passing some spare time is to drop into the National Gallery and to spend 15 or 20 minutes looking closely at a single Cezanne painting. One of the pleasures of this is the sense of shared experience – like going to the cinema or a concert. It is uplifting to be in a building with strangers having similar cultural experiences. In contrast some people prefer to look at a painting in silent isolation. Personally, I find that this experience makes me uncomfortably self-conscious. I worry that I am upsetting the bored security guard who has nothing better to do than watch me. I'm not fond of Royal Academy-style over-crowding, but I'd rather my museums had a sense of purposeful busyness about them than a stern silence. If I want complete peace and quiet I stay at home and curl up with a book.

Josie Appleton offers an unlikely vision of her perfect museum. It would offer its visitors only minimally interpreted 'raw objects', austerely arranged to avoid any risk of 'visual spectacle'. The primary activity would be 'the critical encounter between the scholar and his raw material' (Appleton's visitors, scholars and museum staff are universally male); children would be banished and visitors would observe 'concentration in stillness'. Labels and exhibits would be expressly designed so that they did not engage audiences too much.

The creation of this unpleasant institution would be aided by the fact that there would be few, if any, administrators or educators, and management skills would be discouraged. Instead scholars, separated 'from the immediate demands of politicians, bureaucrats, and even from the public' would rule the roost, worrying little about anything 'external to the [scholarly] matter in hand'. If the people running these museums managed to get the doors open on Monday morning it is unlikely that they would be disturbed by too many visitors. Appleton's vision for museums is a harsh, ascetic one.

There are a few points on which I agree with her. Certainly some exhibits in some museums are incompetent and others are crass – and she cites some of my particular hates. She also correctly identifies the Museums Association's mistake in claiming to speak for society in its draft code of ethics. She will be reassured to know that a substantial proportion of the over 300 museum staff responding to the draft code made this point. A different form of words will be used in the final version of the code.

I also agree that supporting scholarship is a job for museums. However, this is far from saying that the single most important role of museums is their own scholarship. Making collections and information about them available to scholars based in universities and elsewhere remains an important task. In fact, Appleton gives a misleading view of the founding purposes of museums. In a very real sense the public own the collections. This is why museums have always welcomed a wide range of visitors – from the expert to the mildly curious.

All museums have (and always have had) one thing in common – they are places where collections, usually publicly owned in perpetuity, are gathered together and made accessible to visitors. This is the core of a museum; scholarship is just one part of it. To suggest that taking an interest in 'people' somehow reverses 'the meaning and purpose of the museum' is absurd.

One of Appleton's worst misrepresentations is to claim 'exhibitions on African art or slavery' are seen by museums primarily as of interest to 'black British communities'. The exhibitions on slavery mounted by museums in Liverpool and Bristol should not be dismissed in this way. They both have substantial scholarly content and they perform an important function for the whole local population in giving calm, reasoned public exposure to an often misunderstood, misrepresented and manipulated aspect of their cities' histories.

What, then, is Appleton's problem with modern museums? Fundamentally I think it's just a matter of personal taste. Appleton, evidently, likes to 'read books for hours on end' and enjoys 'contemplation in stillness' (I love that phrase – it conjures up images of trying to read a book while trying to maintain a precarious yoga position). She hates videos (I rather like the one she ridicules at Verulamium Museum) and doesn't like to have a 'helpdesk'. In fact, she doesn't seem very keen on doing much except encountering 'raw objects'.

Appleton need not worry. Almost every museum, as she knows, has hundreds, even thousands, of 'raw objects' on show – and no one is forcing her to use the 'helpdesk' or read the labels.

In museums you can – and often do – have it all. Consider a real visit to a modern museum – rather than an Appleton parody. Recently I spent a day at the Natural History Museum. Much of the time I looked at wonderful specimens, assisted by well-written labels and skilfully planned displays. (Incidentally, these good displays are the result of years of careful audience research by the museum.) I had some questions and was pleased to find a helpful member of staff (no doubt an 'educator') who gently pointed out that I had confused ichthyosaurs with coelacanths. He also encouraged me to handle a fossilised dinosaur vertebra, which did much to encourage me to read more when I got home. I even spent some time playing a computer game that taught the basics about how birds are adapted for different environments – a subject I'd never considered before. Thousands of visitors were spending their free time doing similar things. No doubt some of them, particularly children, had been tempted to visit the museum by the promise of an interactive, animatronic monster, but they had all moved on to more serious matters. Elsewhere in the museum, curators were concentrating hard on researching fossil reptiles – and elsewhere in the world museum curators were on field trips making new discoveries.

Appleton's mistake is to assume that her Spartan tastes are shared by the rest of the public. Her prescription of adult-only, object-only museums would be a medicine far more ghastly than today's museums, which at least are dedicated to helping people understand their collections.

A challenge to the new orthodoxy

Charles Saumarez Smith

I have been intrigued by the response of the museum profession to the range of cultural issues, which have been raised by the Institute of Ideas over the last two years. This response was evident at a conference held at the British Museum in July 2000, and then in articles in the Museums Journal addressing arguments put by Josie Appleton.

At one of the sessions held at the British Museum, a group of the leading figures in the museums' world was assembled on the podium. The group included the Director of the Museums Association, Mark Taylor, the then recently appointed Director of *Re:source*, Neville Mackay, and the chair of the Association of Independent Museums, Sam Mullins. What was evident in the papers – it did not need to be pointed out – was the extreme homogeneity of attitude of the new establishment, the belief that they were still battling against an old, entrenched curatorial orthodoxy and that the current agenda for museums should be essentially social and political: broadening audiences, extending education, combating social exclusion.

The audience was diverse in its composition: young and old, professional and lay, some curators, people with a general interest in museums – in other words, not unlike the normal audience for many museums, reasonably well educated and with a set of engaged cultural and historical interests. They were united in their hostility to what was being said. And the hostility came not from the more obviously reactionary figures who were present. It looked as if museums, which traditionally have been treated as sites for the deepening of historical knowledge, had been hijacked by a smooth-talking bureaucracy for essentially political purposes. I felt slightly like someone sitting in the back row of a gathering just before the velvet revolution, because there was so little in common between speakers and audience. On the one hand, those with power and influence in setting the agenda for museums, believe that it is a self-evident truth that they should be used as instruments of social amelioration. On the other hand, those who use museums and visit them don't want them to be used instrumentally. They want them to be open-ended, under-programmed places for individual experience. They want them to be places of history and culture and public education. They don't want them to be patronising. They don't mind if museums are about subjects that they don't fully understand. That is why they come to them.

The official response from the museum profession to this debate so far has been dismissive, if not contemptuous. Instead of welcoming the ideas of a group of activists, who come with well-established credentials on the left, instead of being pleased that the Institute of Ideas is opening up debate about the core functions and social responsibilities of museums, the museum profession has tended to dismiss the debate as being irrelevant or reactionary.

The benefit of Josie Appleton's article **Museums for The People?** is that it sets out the terms of the debate quite clearly. On the one hand, you have the current orthodoxies of museum practice, which tend to stress the virtues of audience analysis, of trying to ensure that displays are accessible to children, and of mediating the experience of objects through active interpretation. On the other hand, you have a new counter-argument, that these ideas, now entrenched in the museum profession, are top-down, over-simplistic propagandising; and that the old orthodoxy, which valued specialist, scholarly expertise and the interpretation of the object, should be rehabilitated.

I am broadly in sympathy with this argument. I certainly think the debate is an important one. But I would put in two caveats to Josie Appleton's argument. The first is that there are still examples of displays which are motivated by the traditional belief in the virtues of unmediated display. One has only to climb to the top floor of the Victoria and Albert Museum to find acres of galleries which make no effort whatsoever to interpret their subject matter. The result is profoundly alienating. Objects need to be understood within a broader social, historical and cultural context. I would

accept that it is the duty of the museum, wherever possible, to supply that context.

The second feature of museum politics which is missing from her piece is any interest in the reasons why the museum profession finds itself in the position it does. One of the reasons is the squeeze on local authority funding in the mid-1980s, including rate capping, which put pressure on non-statutory services. Museum professionals found themselves in a position whereby either their museums went into terminal decline, treated as an irrelevance, or they tried to demonstrate their usefulness to a broader social and educational agenda. A whole generation of museum professionals went into battle to demonstrate that museums are not just about the preservation of the past, but have a relevance to the present; they are not just part of the heritage industry, but have broader educational responsibilities; they should not just service a narrow intellectual elite, but have a broader political relevance. One may not like much of what has happened, but there were good reasons for it. Museums adapted in order to survive.

My own attitude towards the issues which Josie Appleton raises is also coloured by the methodology which she reviles: systematic audience analysis. Four years ago, after the Labour victory in May 1997, the National Portrait Gallery was approached by Tony Banks, then Minister for Sport, as to whether or not we would consider an exhibition about portraits of major sporting figures as a way of raising the profile of sport in Britain and opening up the Gallery to non-traditional audiences. It happened that we had a gap in the programme. We discussed the suggestion and all the staff felt that it was a good one. We put a great deal of energy into the project. It was systematically researched and contained wonderful, unfamiliar material from the last two centuries. But, it did not capture the imagination of new audiences as planned. Nobody was prepared to sponsor it, in spite of support from the minister. Those people who are interested in art and history are not necessarily interested in sport. It seems obvious now, but not at the time. Shortly afterwards we did a comparatively traditional exhibition on the portraiture of John Everett Millais, which was motivated by a scholarly interest in the work of a once popular, but now neglected Victorian painter. It had more than double the number of visitors to *British Sporting Heroes*. What this suggests is what Josie Appleton argues: that the public has an appetite for well presented and intellectually challenging museum displays. After the Dome, this is not a case which should have to be made.

In defence of the middle ground

François Matarasso

Debate about culture has grown enormously since 1945, largely as a result of gradual democratisation and adjustments in our thinking demanded by economic, social and scientific change. The nature of culture, its role in our lives, and the proper relationship of democratic states to the cultural activity of its citizens have all become urgent questions. This is surely healthy, since it is through cultural expression that we develop, articulate and question our values. The more we are able to become involved in these processes, on our own terms and in ways we choose, the better for us individually and for our democratic life.

But there is a discernible tendency, in some of these debates, to adopt the established political trick of undermining the centre ground by presenting arguments as binary alternatives: which side are you on? Such polarisation serves all extremes well, ideological or cultural, since it forces people to accept their underlying analysis and swells the number of their adherents; but it is also a dangerous tactic which contributed directly to much of the last century's suffering. My purpose here is therefore to argue for the middle ground which is still where most of us live and where the least damage tends to be done.

Josie Appleton's thesis is an important corrective to some of the thinking now current within museums, though much of this is more tentative than she suggests. Her arguments against a marginalisation of curatorial scholarship, and against simplistic attempts to provide particular social groups with what they are thought to want, are unimpeachable; likewise her defence of rigour, quality and objectivity, and of our right and ability to create our own ways of engaging with objects. The questions she raises about the relationship of politics to museums (and, by implication, to culture generally) are vital and demand more serious responses than the usual appeal to the arm's-length principle.

But in her advocacy of these values, and of a traditional museology more generally, she presents them as inevitable alternatives to other approaches in museum thinking and practice. There is, of course, nothing inevitable about this opposition. There is no reason why a museum cannot try to make itself and its collection more interesting to more people without abandoning rigour, quality and objectivity: to argue otherwise is, in fact, to underestimate the audience just as she argues museums now do.

Certainly, there are examples of poor, unimaginative and

patronising exhibitions developed in the attempt to attract people who do not currently visit museums. That does not mean that the ideal of helping them to discover the pleasure and value of museums is wrong, only that some of the ways in which it is being pursued are misguided.

She is right to highlight the dangers of relativism, but wrong to imply that cultural absolutism is the only alternative. Culture, as the result of human action, is neither absolute nor neutral. It cannot be detached from ethics, either in its creation or in the uses to which it is put. Most of us now accept that how we interpret and value our experience is not the only valid response to existence. We know that other people, with just as much (or as little) integrity and intelligence, have different beliefs, ideas and understandings. We have learnt, for example, that to say that what is in museums has value does not mean that what has value is in museums.

But we do not in consequence abandon our own beliefs: we temper them, living with the possibility that we might be mistaken. People may be less certain of cultural and moral values than they were but, if so, it is because they have more freedom to reach their own conclusions than they did: it doesn't mean that they have stopped believing in either. Integrity, in the postmodern world, no longer depends on unquestioning adherence to the old faith, but on accepting our own responsibility to test faith for ourselves. As the historian Albert Grosser has written: 'Objectivity does not exist. But there is a great difference between those who seek it and those who turn away from it – deliberately or through ignorance of their own determinants, of the internal prism which distorts their perception of others'.

The nineteenth century concept of the museum was forged in the belief that there is absolute truth and that the curator's task is to collect, present and interpret objects in ways which most effectively illuminate that truth for the public. That remains the underlying belief of many people, including many curators, though it tends to wear more up-to-date dress. It is a legitimate and coherent belief – though its authority without a religious interpretation of life remains opaque – but I do not share it.

Equally, I am unconvinced by much of what the museum profession has done in searching for new alternatives. Perhaps because it has tended to focus on new methods of expressing an existing idea and less often on rethinking the idea itself: the Centre for Popular Music in Sheffield, mentioned by Appleton, is an obvious and instructive example.

Between these alternatives, is a vast, varied and complex territory now being explored by our best museums. They are illuminating and trying to understand the world in which we live and our experience of it, but they are finding ways of doing so with the public as much more equal partners than before. In this dialogue, visitors have something to give as well as to receive, museums learn as well as educate. Its success depends on museums articulating clear values, identities and purposes which people can engage with, interrogate and respond to – as do the Eden Project or Walsall Art Gallery. The opposite of 'dumbing down', such leadership demands courage because it does not hide behind feigned authority, but is prepared to seek objectivity while recognising the essential subjectivity of human experience and understanding. It is in this territory that we may find adult forms of museology for an adult world.

The access issue is nothing new

Robert Anderson

'The average attendance at the National Museums and Galleries within the administrative county of London hardly exceeds 100,000 a week. This figure represents a mere fraction of the numbers – probably not less than 3,000,000 - who pour weekly into the London cinemas. Though the forms of recreation offered by Museums and by picture theatres are not comparable, most people would agree that attendances at Museums and Galleries might well be larger.'

Brief Guide to the National Museums and Galleries of London, HMSO 1935

'The major drawback to visiting the [British] museum is people. I guess that the British Museum is on the agenda for a lot of visitors to London who feel they must go, but don't actually much like museums.'

Andrew Wyllie, **London Museums: A Handbook**, 2001

These two views about museum visiting run counter to what might be expected to be the orthodoxy of their times. The author of the 1930s piece, the Rt Hon Viscount D'Abernon, GCB, GCMG, FRS, scarcely confirms our preconceptions about museums of those times being reserved for elite audiences. He goes on to say that with reductions in working hours, it is 'of national importance that this change should result in improved efficiency and development of national culture. The Museums and Galleries can contribute powerfully to a beneficial use of leisure.' On the other hand, Andrew Wyllie's attitude runs sharply counter to the prevailing governmental view of today that for museums, social exclusion is a concern that must be tackled by the national institutions. He goes on to refer to the antisocial behaviour of visitors and the pressure of numbers in the British Museum.

Over the years, many attempts have been made to decide what the primary purposes of museums are, and which audiences they should be serving. The Trustees of the British Museum (the first national institution of its kind) made several statements in the 1750s, for example that the collections were 'for the use and benefit of the publick, who may have free Access to view and peruse the same.' It has often been said that the arrangements in the early British Museum excluded all those other than the ruling classes because of the restricted daytime hours of opening and the complexities of obtaining (free) admission tickets. It is not particularly helpful to project backwards views on access based on present structures of society.

In fact, the British Museum was remarkably accessible for its time. The Statutes and Rules of 1759 pointed out that the institution was intended for general users as well as for scholars: 'tho' chiefly designed for the use of learned and studious men, both natives and foreigners, in their researches into the several parts of knowledge, yet being a national establishment... it may be judged reasonable, that the advantages accruing from it should be rendered as general as possible.' This is reinforced by a grumpy 1780s report from staff who reported that they had 'to answer all the Questions of forty different Persons, from the mechanic up to the first Scholar and Person of Quality in the Kingdom.' A visitor of 1782, Carl Philip Moritz, felt it worthwhile recording: 'The visitors were of all classes and both sexes, including some of the lowest class; for, since the Museum is the property of the nation, everyone must be allowed the right of entry.' What should be noticed from this evidence is that who exactly was coming to the museum is a matter of comment.

Throughout the 19th Century, the British Museum made it more and more easy for working people to attend. The need for tickets was abolished in 1805, and the requirement that guides accompany parties was dropped five years later. From 1837, the Museum opened on some public holidays. Accessibility to museums did not originate as an issue in the 1990s, as some would have us think.

What is on offer to museum visitors and how it is presented is also a matter which has been debated over a considerable period. This was a matter of interest to the 1860 Select Committee. Henry Cole, then Superintendent of the South Kensington Museum, was questioned closely by unconvinced commissioners about the benefits of the Food Museum, which formed part of the complex of collections. He defended the collection in these terms, 'It is very hard to say what advantage the public derive from anything in a metaphysical point of view; but as all human knowledge is supposed to be useful, I cannot doubt that knowledge as connected with food is useful.' On being pressed on the matter, he persisted, 'I should say that after the pictures, which is the most popular collection, the food collection is the next most popular.'

There was also much debate about the function of the proto-Science Museum: should it be based on the historical collections, showing the state of science as the current point on a continuum of development, or should the historical matter be suppressed, and contemporary science be displayed in museums without its ancestry? In recent decades, there is no doubt that presenting the science through the medium of its antiquities has lost out. There is now a strong tendency to emphasise the benefits of recent science in a triumphalist manner. Often the material culture of science is an unimportant part of display, or even absent, with demonstrations and texts dominating. The assets of some museums are simply not utilised when new approaches are instituted. Surely, if this approach is to continue, scientific antiquities should be made available to history museums, so that a more rounded and balanced view of our cultural past can be presented.

With this change of emphasis, the kind of people museums need to employ is not likely to be those whose scholarly interests are object-based. In large museums, it is those with marketing and communications skills who are best able to deal with currently fashionable approaches. In small museums, there are now such funding crises that it is unlikely that staff will have any highly specialised knowledge; it is often a struggle just to keep such places open. There are strong arguments to keep the lamp of scholarship burning in a few museums with rich collections, even if this approach cannot be universal. In fact, there are strong arguments in favour of a mixed museum economy. Let us have the science centres, the interactive demonstrations and so on, but they do not need to be in expensive buildings in city centres. Our object-based museums should optimise their assets in thought-provoking ways, by showing how material culture can provide unique sources of evidence for the past.

At the heart of civic society

Timothy Mason

There are over two thousand museums in the United Kingdom. I am not sure that many of them, large or small, would recognise Josie Appleton's lengthy vostra culpa or her view of their apocalyptic decline into a melting pot of 'cultural leftism' or 'intellectual nihilism'. Except, perhaps, in one regard – it is true that they are, for the most part, 'guilty' of trying to attract growing numbers through their collective doors – and with notable success. The hundred million visits made to museums in this country each year have made museum and gallery visiting one of the nation's most popular leisure time activities.

In his charming but thoughtful book *Museums and Art Galleries*, published in 1888, Thomas Greenwood tells of a visit to a 'local Museum... situated in some narrow or unfrequented street, or some out-of-the-way yard'. Up the stairs 'dust and disorder [are] reigning supreme... The orderly soul of the Museum student will quake at the sight of a Chinese lady's boot encircled by a necklace made of shark's teeth, or a helmet of one of Cromwell's soldiers grouped with some Roman remains. Another corner may reveal an Egyptian mummy placed in a medieval chest... the cups of a crack cricketer of the county... or even the stuffed

relics of a pet pug dog.' I am sure we can all recall museums like this but said Greenwood, 'that order and system is coming out of chaos in many Museums is clear... Museums are becoming institutions of far reaching utility and the pride of all intelligent citizens.'

More than a century later, there are but few museums that have not sought to make themselves more and more relevant to the world in which we live and the public they serve. Museums, says Charles Landry, are now situated in the 'heart of civic society', in his metaphorical 'public square, along with the church, the market and the town hall', and offering an ideal 'neutral territory', a safe haven for the consideration of ideas. Few museum staff would now argue against the need for museums to play a part in their communities, and within a changing social context.

If museums in Britain are about anything, they are collectively about everything – from moon rock to trams, from literature to manufacturing, from sport to fine art. Whatever they may collect, they share a recognition of the supremacy of the object and, despite Josie Appleton's fears, it is objects with which museums continue to be primarily concerned. What makes museums and galleries so special is that at their heart is the object, where the real thing, three dimensional and authentic, can be admired, studied and interpreted. As Dillon Ripley, then Secretary of the Smithsonian Institution, wrote in 1970, 'in this brave new world of ours, perhaps only objects which inherently possess truth can teach truth. An object to be touched, seen, felt and smelled is true. Furthermore it is a source of data, part of the only data bank we possess.'

Collections bring with them responsibilities. Objects not only represent our past in the present, they give us a responsibility to conserve them for the future. Most museum directors have, however, long recognised the need to manage with a skilful political hand, which balances the public face of the museum's work with the scholarship, research, conservation, documentation, and safe and responsible storage, upon which a museum depends but which all too often attracts little publicity or recognition.

As often as not, these are the people's collections, held in public ownership. At the heart of any discussion about museums in a community context lies the word access – one of those late 20th century words which, like community itself, has been burdened with a multitude of interpretations. In recent years we have moved beyond simple availability – questions of physical, intellectual and sensory access – to a broader concept of accessibility, embracing education, social inclusion, cultural diversity and the internet.

Museums have responded positively to these issues – not as Josie Appleton suggests by allowing the importance of the collection to decline – but by increasing access to their collections and to their work, placing both the museum and its

collections very much in the centre of the community, however defined. Not only have many museums worked hard to increase attendance, they have also sought to attract a public far more representative of the communities they serve.

They have sought to give a fresh interpretation to the objects in their care. They have opened their stores and conservation studios to the public and used information technology as a means of encouraging wider access to their collections. They have expanded their publication programmes and developed their education activities in lively and imaginative ways. They have formed links with sectors of the community who do not traditionally use museums, and developed projects for disadvantaged groups. Museums of all sizes have played a significant part in economic regeneration and tourism – look, for example, at what has happened on London's South Bank, Liverpool's Docks, on Tyne and Wear, in Walsall and Salford.

For the local museum, the very act of recording and presenting a local story, through archaeology, social and industrial history, topographical works of art, natural sciences, places them at the centre of their community. Local people and local place are the source of the museum's collections, and the contextual information which makes sense of them. It is the main audience for whatever they offer – exhibitions, events, and education.

Museums that have presented their work within such contexts and against such a background of activity have found it easier to answer the more difficult questions about their contemporary relevance and to counter tired arguments about elitism. Museums at the heart of the community have found themselves to be very much in tune with current priorities.

Museums have indeed 'put the perceived needs of the people at the heart of [their] work' and in doing so have placed themselves and their collections firmly in the 21st century.

Scholars, curators and politicians

David Barrie

Josie Appleton's claim that the 'scholar-curator', and even the museum object, are endangered species may not be new, but seldom have the arguments been so trenchantly expressed. The root causes of the malaise are to be found, she suggests, in the spread of a shallow kind of 'cultural relativism' in museum and academic circles, and the political triumph of free market economics. This part of her argument is persuasive enough, but the case she makes for reasserting the primacy of collections is weakened by oversimplification and overstatement.

To maintain that museums should concern themselves only with the preservation, display and study of objects is to brush aside the fundamental reason why museums and galleries were originally established. As she admits, 'the central concern of curators' at museums like the Louvre was 'the collection, preservation and study of objects deemed to be of artistic, historic or scientific interest'. But she fails to look behind these words. Objects were not collected just for the amusement of the curators. They were collected because they were thought to be of interest to the 'public', and because it was believed (and still is by many) that contact with such objects could have an intellectually, morally and spiritually uplifting effect. This is precisely what we mean when we say that museums can inspire people.

It is therefore a wild exaggeration to claim that 'Turning museums towards The People... is a total reversal of [their] meaning and purpose ... and puts in question the existence of museums as such'. No reasonable definition of the word 'People' supports the contention that those in charge of museums and galleries have ever been, or now should be, careless of what 'The People' want or need. The truth is that a good curator has always been both a scholar and a communicator. To accumulate knowledge without actively seeking to share it is misguided in any circumstances, and quite simply parasitic if done at the taxpayer's expense. But actively to reach out and offer the public the chance to share your knowledge, your enthusiasm, your love of the objects in your care – that is to be a real curator.

It is for this reason that we should be cautious about dismissing the use of new methods of interpretation in museums and galleries, such as the revealing video installations in the new African displays at the British Museum. Nor should we criticise museum professionals for attempting to find out more about their audiences. There is nothing patronising or 'disdainful' about trying – with respect and humility – to find out why some people hesitate to visit a museum, or whether those people who do visit find the experience boring or even intimidating. Good curators can find ways of tackling some of these problems without prostituting themselves in the process. They should not expect everyone to share their tastes and interests, but they should at least try to help them do so.

The danger of emphasising the preservation, display and study of collections to the exclusion of all else is that we risk falling into a kind of chilly intellectual snobbery that says to the public: 'This is my collection, not yours. I know far more about it than you ever will and I don't care what you think of it. Learn from me if you want, but only on my terms. Otherwise, watch **Eastenders**.' Luckily for all of us, such arrogance is now becoming rare among museum professionals.

On the other hand, as Appleton rightly points out, many museum curators are now bending too far in the other direction. It is a cruel irony that by concentrating all their resources on trying to become successful visitor attractions, some museums have betrayed the collections that alone justify their existence. Although this is lamentable, Appleton is perhaps too hard on the curators who have fallen into this trap. The real culprits are the politicians who, having failed to grasp that museums are valuable in themselves, have insisted that in return for state funding they must help deliver political goals like social inclusion or urban renewal. Divided and uncertain, and so lacking the unity and strength to stand up to this threat, many museums have rushed to embrace the government's agenda. But they have done so primarily out of need. Struggling with growing deficits and collapsing morale, they have had very little choice.

The philistine 'instrumental' view of the purpose and value of museums is beguiling but insidious. So long as the government keeps on forking out, everything may seem fine. But sooner or later it is possible – perhaps even likely – that, having tried the experiment, it will find better or more cost-effective ways of achieving its political objectives and turn its back on museums. By then it may be too late for those who care to convince their political paymasters – and the voters whose views they monitor so closely – that museums are intrinsically valuable and worth funding properly for that reason alone.

So while museums are busy ticking off their completed government performance targets, the crucial arguments for their proper and sustained state funding are being forgotten. And by failing to press their case on their own unique merits, museums are leaving themselves dangerously exposed. Unless this trend is reversed, the future of the 'scholar-curator', and indeed of many museum collections, will look bleak. That is the greatest challenge now facing the museum community.

Reply –

Josie Appleton

The purpose of this essay was to examine, and to criticise, the new political agenda that now dominates museum policy. The essence of this new agenda is that museums should look beyond their traditional roles and seek their rationale in something external to themselves. This external rationale is The People.

Some respondents claim that I overstate my case. Yes, if I were giving a snapshot of the state of museums today, I would be. But what I presented was a trend, and the argument that if this trend continued, the museum as we have known it has no future. That much is in fact the least contentious part of my essay. Almost any reasonably intelligent or insightful observer, whether he approves or not, will agree that what is happening now in museums will lead to their fundamental transformation. Yes, there are still plenty of 'traditional' museums around, but that is mainly due to lack of money. This transformation will take time. But when the money is available, you get the likes of the £50million Wellcome Wing opened last year at the Science Museum. This embodies all the trends I describe – sidelining the collection, interactive gizmos, manipulating the visitors.

What is distinctive in what I said is, in the first place, that 'The People that [museums] are so anxious to follow are a pure projection', an ideological fantasy of the cultural elite itself. Those who say I create a false dichotomy between objects and the people are making a simple categorical confusion. As I clearly state in my essay, 'The People' and the public are not the same thing. The public exists, The People

do not. The one has a real existence, independent of the elite, the other is created by the elite to serve its own interests. Duty to The People is a spurious, self-serving duty, allowing the elite to do what it likes. Duty to the public imposes real demands of intellectual honesty, rigour and integrity. But that sense of honour is ultimately just an extension of the curator's own intellectual sense of duty. In other words, a good curator would no more deceive others than he would himself. Objects and the public go together perfectly. Objects and The People don't.

But although there is no conflict of interest between the study and display of objects, the two things are distinct – which is why I argued that scholars 'must be allowed to study their subject… without having to wonder all the time whether it is directly relevant to the public'. A fraction of museums' knowledge about their collections becomes part of public exhibitions, just as a fraction of academics' knowledge goes into lectures. To develop this knowledge, curators should be free to pursue collection scholarship beyond immediate utility for exhibitions. Sue Millar may be right when she says that curators of the past often shirked their responsibility to display and interpret their collections. But that is why, rather than confining scholarship to the ivory tower or dusty archive, and leaving the public galleries to PR specialists, we should expect our curators to combine dedication to their subject with attention to how the collections are displayed.

The second distinctive point I made was that once a museum is no longer organised around its collection, it loses its reason for existence. A collection creates its own rational order which fosters a spirit of learning and intellectual enthusiasm. Once obligations are imposed on a museum which have nothing to do with its core activity, it becomes a sort of generic institution, providing a host of services which could just as easily be provided by other institutions. The original function becomes an ancillary one serving the new generic ones. David Lowenthal writes that I 'continually assert but never coherently [explain] why artefacts have an overarching value as museums' "core functions"'. This statement reveals the depths of the problem. I would no more attempt to explain such a thing than I would attempt to explain why a hospital should concentrate on curing the sick or a school on educating the young. Lowenthal is right in one respect: the accusations I level at museums could be levelled at other institutions. Almost every public body which once devoted itself to a specific function is increasingly charged with other generic functions such as fighting social exclusion, changing attitudes and lifestyles, promoting awareness about something or other, improving self-esteem. We may only be at the beginning of this process. Perhaps it's only a matter of time before museums start offering personal financial services.

Possibly I was not clear enough on some issues. I had no intention of arguing that museums should only display great works of art; rather, that people should go to museums to see unusual objects, not things they can see in the shops. Today, with the fetish of ordinariness and relevance, any artefact distant from everyday experience is presumed to be potentially alienating, rather than interesting. The everyday objects of the past, such as those exhibited in the Geffrye or Petrie museums, are not the everyday objects of today.

Taken alone, I cannot think of a single innovation that has taken place in museums in recent years to which I object. I have no objection in principle to marketing, helpdesks, interactive exhibits, or any other aspect of new museum practice. If some use can be found for these things in communicating the collection to the public, then they should be used. The problem is that the growth of these services is out of all proportion to their real utility. In most cases, their use has compounded the loss of focus which often led to their introduction in the first place.

Many of the views attributed to me are so manifestly absurd that I assume the reader will recognise them as such. That I want children banned from museums, that visitors should observe objects in silence, that museums should be for the amusement of curators, and so on. Maurice Davies is the master of these absurdities. One in particular does require clarification: the charge that I want objects to be shown in the raw, without interpretation.

I stated clearly that museums should always interpret their collections, and re-interpret them. Historical and cultural research should be conveyed to the public as clearly and succinctly as possible. That objects have a context and that interpretation involves judgement doesn't mean that curators need retreat into a relativistic 'dialogue' with visitors. Curators spend their lives studying the collection and should take responsibility for its interpretation. That does not mean the visitor cannot draw his own conclusions. Curiously, a new tendency towards object fetishism has begun to emerge recently with the devaluing of scholarship. Instead of providing genuine historical context and interpretation, museums offer emotional engagement with objects, allowing the visitor to feel and touch. Not bad in itself, but an abdication of responsibility by the museum when it replaces real interpretation. A variation on this is the call by some to empty the storerooms and put everything on display without adequate interpretation.

Finally, there is the question, raised by David Barrie, of whether 'the real culprits are [not curators but] the politicians who, having failed to grasp that museums are valuable in themselves, have insisted that in return for state funding they must help deliver political goals like social inclusion or urban renewal'. Of course, the imposition of government targets is lamentable. But Barrie himself points out that museums are 'divided and uncertain, and... lacking the unity and strength to stand up to this threat'. Instead of satisfying himself with this observation, he might have served his case better to ask why this was the case. It is unfortunate that politicians fail to recognise the unique value of museums; but how could we expect them to, when museums cannot recognise it for themselves?